DISNEP PRESENTS A **PIXAR** FILM

The Essential Guide

Written by Simon Jowett

Contents

Introduction

ightning McQueen looks set to be the first rookie ever to win the Piston Cup Championship. But this self-confident young hotshot's dreams of fame and fortune take a wrong turn when he ends up in the sleepy backwater of Radiator Springs, a once-vibrant town on the famous Highway 66....

Highway 66 was once a major route across the US – until the newly built Interstate took away all the traffic. With so few travellers passing through, poor Radiator Springs has fallen on hard times.

When McQueen's arrival wreaks havoc on the main street, the red-hot race car with the lucky lightning bolt is sentenced to repair the damaged road. While McQueen works on the road, he gets to know the easy-livin' folks of Radiator Springs—and learns that there's more to life than winning....

Lightning McQueen

Lightning McQueen is a hotshot race car who's poised to become the first rookie ever to win the Piston Cup. The racing sensation came into the season unknown, but everyone knows him now! McQueen only has two things on his mind: winning and the perks that come with it, including a big sponsorship from Dinoco.

McQueen prepares for the race in his deluxe trailer, which has a lit trophy wall.

McQueen has a special way of avoiding a pile up during the Dinoco 400 – he even manages to wink at his adoring fans as he leaps by. *Ka-chow!!!*

CAR FACTS

Lightning McQueen has a supercharged V-8 engine and can reach 200 mph (322 kph). His racing wheels are fitted with special Lightyear racing tyres.

McQueen thinks the Rust-eze guys are bad for his image, even though they gave him his first big break.

A Sizzling Solo Performance

On the race track, McQueen taunts the other cars and is impatient with his pit crew. In fact, he's fired three crew chiefs this season already. However, that doesn't bother McQueen, who says he's a 'one-man show'.

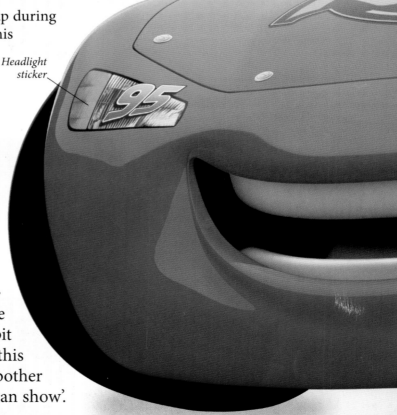

Headlight sticker

Dedicated Driver

Mack is McQueen's loyal driver, willing to drive through the night in order to get his boss to the next race as fast as possible. In the racing world, Mack is McQueen's one true friend.

Lucky lightning bolt

Free-flowing dual exhaust

The King

A racing legend, Strip Weathers is known simply as The King. He has won more Piston Cup Championships than any other car in history, but he has achieved something even more amazing – he hasn't let it go to his head. It's his last racing season, and he'd love to retire with one last Piston Cup to add to his collection.

The wealthy Dinoco oil company grabs attention with its glitzy tent and a fancy helicopter.

The Prize

The King has been sponsored by Dinoco for many years. As he is about to retire, his competitors in the Dinoco 400 race all want a piece of the fame and fortune that a Dinoco sponsorship could bring them.

CAR FACTS

The King's 'Corporation Blue' paint job always stands out in a crowd. During his glory days, The King's mighty 426 HEMI engine reached speeds of 200 mph (322 kph).

Rear spoiler keeps The King firmly on the race track at high speeds

The King's wife has always been the veteran race car's biggest fan. Win or lose, The King is always her champion.

Lightyear racing tyres

The King And McQueen

The King can see that Lightning McQueen has the talent and ability to win the Piston Cup – but he's got a lot to learn. The arrogant young race car needs to find out there's a whole lot more to racing than just winning.

The Fast Lane

The King may be a veteran, but he's no pushover – as Chick Hicks finds out again. The King takes the lead in the Dinoco 400 while Chick chews on his exhaust fumes.

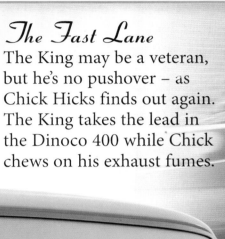

Dinoco logo – the mark of a champion

Chick Hicks

Dream Sponsor
Chick dreams of landing the Dinoco sponsorship and schmoozing with Tex Dinoco, the head of the mighty oil company.

A veteran of the racing circuit, Chick Hicks would go a lot faster without all those chips on his shoulder. He has bumped and cheated his way to more second places than any car in history, always finishing as runner-up to the The King. Now that The King is about to retire, Chick is sure that this is his chance to be a winner – whatever it takes.

Beady eyes

Chick's official sponsor: Hostile Takeover Bank

High-visibility advertising space

McQueen nicknames Chick 'Thunder' – as thunder always comes after lightning!

Chick is a ruthless competitor who doesn't mind giving his rivals a little nudge!

Chick's Tricks

From the moment the Dinoco 400 starts, Chick is looking for a way to bump himself to the front. He is out to stop McQueen at any cost, as the rookie poses a threat to Chick's dreams of racing glory.

CAR FACTS

Chick Hicks's specifications are pretty much the same as Lightning McQueen's, but his V-8 engine is slightly less powerful... hence his uncontrollable need to cheat!

When the Dinoco 400 is declared a three-way draw, Chick is happy to get another chance to prove it's time for a new era – 'the Chick era'. *Ka-Chick-a!*

Mean Machine

For Chick, life is all about what's on the surface. He may be covered in sponsor stickers, but the only one he really wants is Dinoco.

Chick's bumper gets a lot of use with all his bumping

Moustache

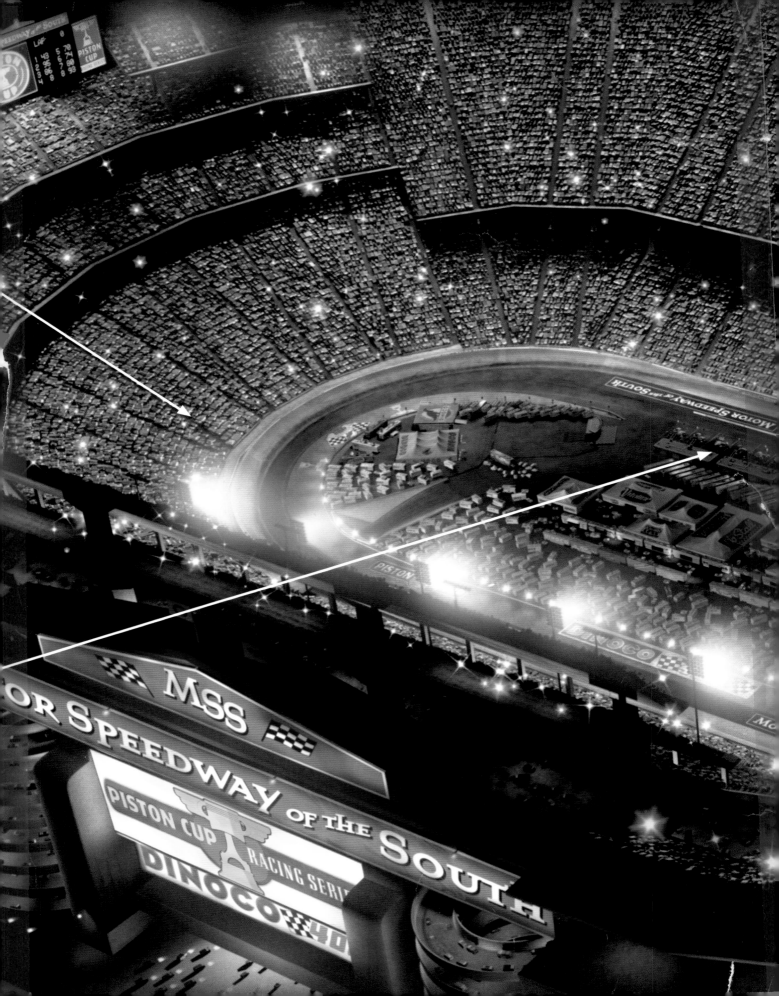

The Speedway

The Dinoco 400 is held at the Motor Speedway of the South, home of the final race in the Piston Cup Racing Series. This is the most hotly anticipated race of the whole season, with tickets selling out in record time. The stadium is packed to the rafters with eager, revved-up race fans ready to cheer on their favourite racer!

Twins Mia and Tia are McQueen's biggest fans. All McQueen has to do is flash his lucky lightning bolt to make them faint with excitement.

Chick's Crew

Key contender Chick Hicks relies on his pit crew. When he pulls into the pit for a high-speed wheel change, the crew moves like a well-oiled machine, changing his tyres, cleaning his windshield and refuelling him for the final, most vital few laps of the race.

It's all gas 'n' goes for McQueen when he ignores his pit crew's advice to change his tyres – a decision he lives to regret!

Dinoco 400

The Dinoco 400 is the final race in the Piston Cup Championship and the gateway to the kind of fame and fortune most cars can only dream of. Heading into the race, three race cars are tied for the season point lead – The King, Chick Hicks and Lightning McQueen. Whoever wins the race wins the championship!

Talk the Talk

Smooth-talking Bob Cutlass and excitable, shoot-from-the-lip Darrel Cartrip are the commentators for this historic day in racing. Their oil pressure is through the roof with excitement!

The pace car leads the racers during warm-up laps, accidents and re-starts. When the pace car pulls off the track, the race is on!

On Track

Forty-three racers tear around the track, but only one will be crowned the winner.

Green means 'go', yellow means 'caution' and white means 'last lap'... but every car longs to be the first to see the winning checkered flag!

On the Road

DJ, Boost, Snot Rod and Wingo are four pumped-up pranksters who think they're better than every other car on the road. Loaded down with spoilers, speakers, superchargers, extra lights and attitude, they love to roam the Interstate at night, terrorising unsuspecting cars and trucks.

The gang cruises the Interstate late at night, weaving in and out of traffic and looking for 'nodders'.

DJ sports tweeters, woofers, sub-woofers and enough lights to illuminate a small town.

DJ

DJ likes his music super-loud, but he'll switch to easy-listening lullabies to send Mack to sleep. He believes his beat really can't be beat!

Boost loves to show off his trick carbon fibre panels.

Boost

He's the leader of the pack with a paint job that looks like a million dollars – but that's not even half of what Boost thinks he's worth!

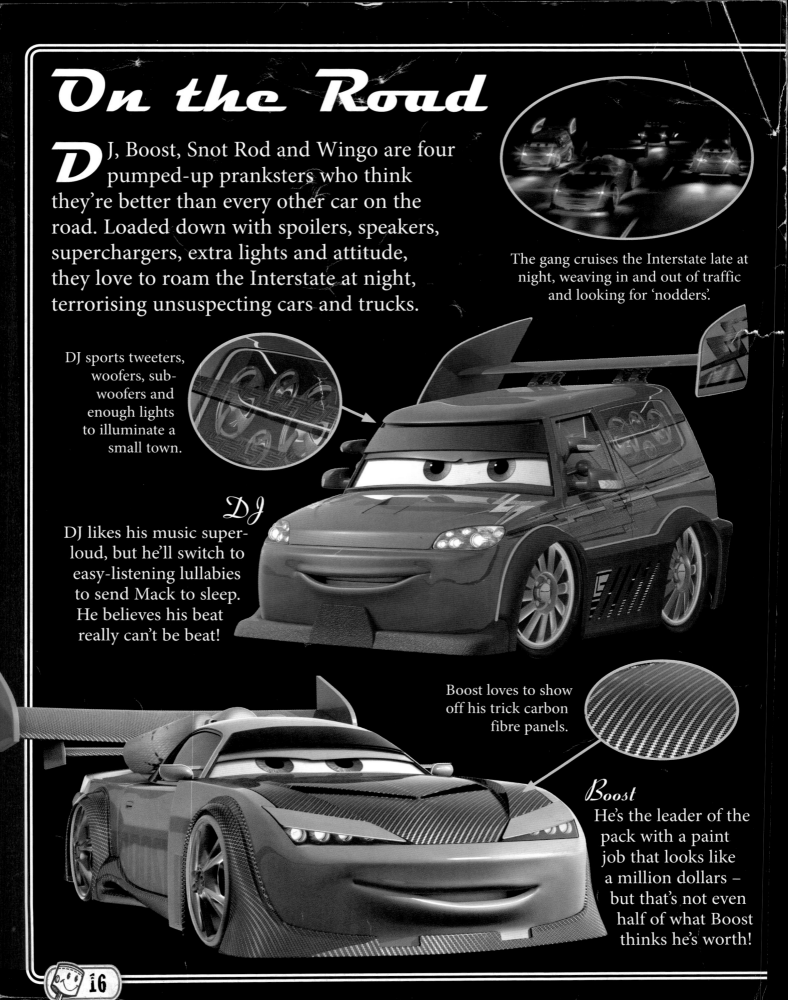

Lane Change, Man

The gang spots Mack dozing off on the Interstate as he drives to the Piston Cup tie-breaker. As they playfully bump him across the road, they have no idea that Mack's precious cargo, McQueen, falls out the back!

Snot Rod is proud of his custom grille logo.

Snot Rod

Snot Rod is a muscle car with an overcharged supercharger which makes him the fastest and least predictable of the gang. When he sneezes, fire shoots out of his exhaust... and he shoots off course!

When Wingo switches on his headlights, every other car reaches for its sun visor!

Wingo

Wingo's spoilers pressed him any closer to the road, he'd be flat! His swooping side and front panels make it hard o tell where he ends and the road begins!

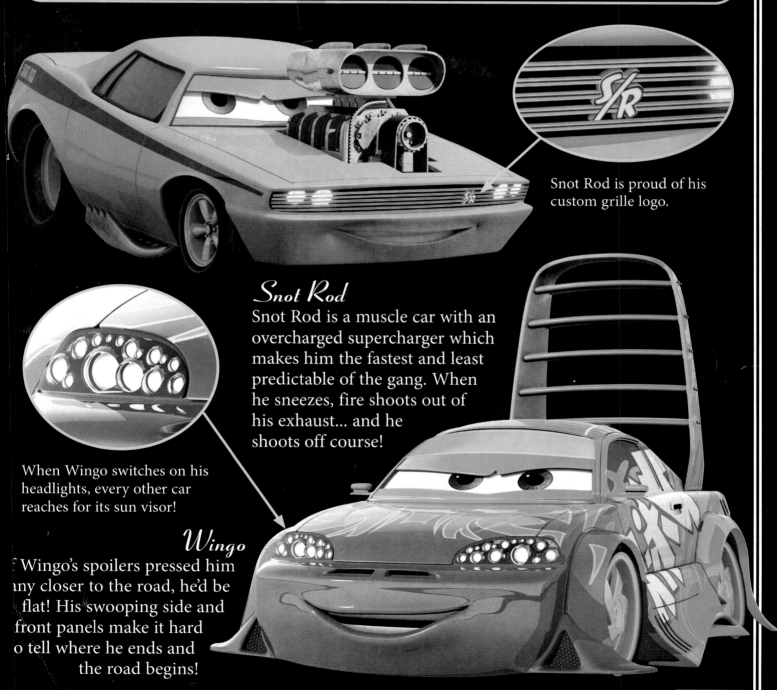

Mater

Owner of the fastest tow-rope in Radiator Springs, Mater always sees the bright side of any situation. Even after Lightning McQueen tears up the main street, Mater just sees it as an opportunity to make a new friend.

As manager of the town impound, it's Mater's job to tow McQueen to the courthouse for damaging the main road.

Good Ol' Boy
Mater runs Tow Mater Towing and Salvage and manages the local impound. One day he's hoping to find his hood again!

Pronounced like 'tuh-mater' but without the 'tuh'

The fastest tow-rope in Carburetor County!

When McQueen promises to get Mater a ride in a helicopter, Mater declares McQueen is his best friend.

Back to Back
Mater claims he is the world's best backwards driver. As he says, he doesn't need to know where he's going, just where he's been. He offers to teach McQueen how to drive backwards… maybe he can use it in his big race?

CAR FACTS

Mater's suspension may be a little rusty, and his crusty cab may have seen better days, but his sunny disposition and reliable V-8 engine keep the old tow truck running smoothly.

Mater likes McQueen right away, but doesn't hesitate to tell his new buddy that he owes him $32,000 in legal fees!

Rear-view mirrors help Mater with his backwards driving skills

Trusty V-8 engine

Mismatched tyres

Tractor Tipping

To liven up the quiet days and long nights in Radiator Springs, Mater has his own way of having fun – tractor tipping! Late one night, Mater takes McQueen out to a field of sleeping tractors and dares him to join in....

HONK! Mater startles a sleeping tractor so it falls over backwards.

King of the Field

Mater warns McQueen not to wake up Frank, but forgets to mention that Frank is ten tons of angry agricultural machinery who doesn't take kindly to anyone messing with his tractors.

Frank's blades chew up wheat, grass – whatever's in his way!

On the Run

Only one thing can spoil the tractor-tipping fun, and that's Frank the Combine! When Frank comes after Mater and McQueen, they do what any car would do – RUN!

Frank swings out his funnel when he's ready to off-load his harvest.

McQueen agrees with Mater – tractor tipping is fu-un!

Every tractor has a different spot pattern.

Exhaust pipe makes an awful funny sound when a tractor is tipped over!

Down on the Farm

Tractors are dozy, docile and dopey. They love sleeping after a hard day's work chewing up the fields, which makes them easy targets for a certain tow truck's mischievous antics.

Sally

Sally sports a little pinstripe tattoo underneath her rear wing.

A sleek, high-powered, modern sports car from California, Sally took the off-ramp from life in the fast lane and found the peace and beauty she was looking for in Radiator Springs. She fell in love with the town and the surrounding countryside, and is determined to do everything she can to put Radiator Springs back on the map.

Stuttgart styling provides Sally's smooth sports-car curves

Lightweight alloy wheels

McQueen is not just accused – he's guilty!

Mater offers to be McQueen's lawyer

As Radiator Springs' town attorney, Sally has a strong sense of justice. She is determined that McQueen should fix the road he ruined.

CAR FACTS

Sally is a real road rocket! Her rear-engine 3596cc flat-6 gives her a top speed of 177 mph (285kph). She's built for life in the fast lane, but finds a slower pace of life more to her liking.

Sally runs the Cozy Cone Motel, which she lovingly restored to its former glory. Her office displays her caution cone collectibles.

When Sally gives McQueen a full tank of gas, everyone wonders if he'll run for it. But Sally trusts him – she wants to show him that sometimes it's good to slow down.

Drive Time
Sally values the history of Highway 66, the Mother Road. As she says, "cars didn't drive on it to make good time. They drove on it to have great times."

Doc Hudson

The smooth-riding Hudson Hornet known to Radiator Springs' residents as 'Doc' runs the local medical clinic and serves as the town judge. He doesn't like noise or fuss and his low-gear charm has won the townsfolk's respect. But Doc has a high-speed secret in his past that he's willing to do (almost) anything to protect!

Doc runs the Ornament Valley Mechanical Clinic and looks after the health of every car in Radiator Springs.

The Daily Exhaust — FINAL

CRASH!
HUDSON HORNET OUT FOR SEASON

Season Ender Fender Bender Puts Young Hornet In Garage

Doc's racing career ended after he was badly damaged in a crash. By the time he was repaired, the fickle racing world told him "you're history".

Doc's sleek exterior hides a race-winning Twin 'H' powerhouse

When Doc sports his red racing tyres, his awesome skills can help him manoeuvre even the trickiest of turns.

Glory Days

Plain-speaking and low-riding, no one in town knows about Doc's former life as 'The Fabulous Hudson Hornet', when he lived the race car lifestyle to the full. Although he never talks about his racing days, Doc still likes to take a spin around Willys Butte when he thinks no one is looking.

Shiny chrome grille

Judge Hudson

As well as looking after the townsfolk's health, Doc also looks after the law in Radiator Springs, as the firm-but-fair town judge. At first, Doc tries to run McQueen out of town – he believes an untrusty race car like McQueen is the last thing the town needs.

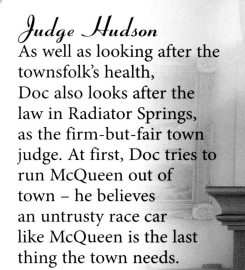

CAR FACTS

Combined with his race-equipped straight-6 flathead engine, capable of putting out 175 horsepower, Doc's low centre of gravity helps make him a formidable race car.

Chrome, chrome and... more chrome!

The Race

Determined to get out of Radiator Springs, McQueen completes the road repairs in an hour... but he does such a bad job that Doc demands he scrape it up and start over. When McQueen refuses, Doc makes him an offer: If the race car can beat Doc in a contest at Willys Butte, he can forget about the road and go free.

Sheriff lays down the law to the two competitors: "No bumpin', no cheatin', no spittin', no bitin', no road rage, no shovin', no oil-slickin', no road-hoggin', no lollygaggin."

The Start Line

"I am speed," McQueen tells himself, as he does before every race, revving his powerful engine. Doc's engine coughs and grinds feebly. Everybody's sure the race is over before it's begun.

McQueen feels confident that he will win the race. But what McQueen doesn't realise is that this is dirt, not asphalt.

Taillight sticker

Rusteze

Medicated Bumper Ointment

95

Spectator Sport

The cars watch from the clifftop as McQueen streaks away from the start line, leaving Doc standing in the dust. All he has to do is make one lap and the race will be over!

Nobody understands why Doc doesn't move when Luigi waves the flag. But Doc has a plan....

The wily Hudson knows McQueen will take the turn too fast – and sure enough, the unlucky car flies off a cliff and lands in a prickly cactus patch!

Luigi waves the flag... they're off!!

51HHMD

Sheriff

Sheriff is the keeper of the peace in Radiator Springs and takes his job very seriously. When McQueen speeds towards town going way over the speed limit, Sheriff pulls after the crazy hotrodder. Sirens blaring, Sheriff keeps pace until McQueen ends up barrelling into town and causing mayhem!

When McQueen makes a run for it, he runs out of fuel at the Radiator Springs billboard (Sheriff's favourite spot for a nap) where Sheriff and Sally are waiting.

CAR FACTS

Sheriff still runs his original 255cc flathead Police Special V-8. It used to generate 110 horsepower when new. He has slowed down since then, but nobody doubts that Sheriff's word is still law!

Sheriff loves to drop in at Flo's V8 Café to shoot the breeze and tell stories about his days on the old Highway 66.

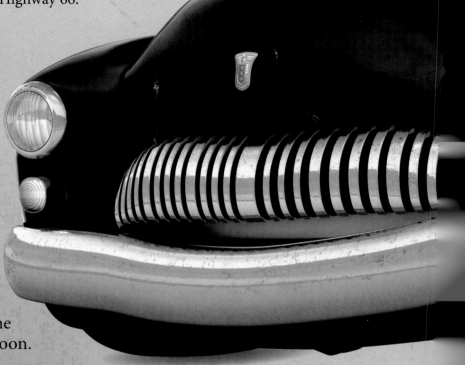

Sheriff's not sure what Doc has in mind when he challenges McQueen to a race, but he'll make sure it's fair.

Keeping In Shape

Thanks to regular check-ups from his old friend Doc Hudson, Sheriff has been keeping Radiator Springs safe for a long time, and he doesn't plan to give up anytime soon.

Paving Partners
McQueen's punishment is to fix the town's road by hauling Bessie, the big, messy paving machine. She belches steam and covers the road (and McQueen!) with hot, sticky tar.

Siren ensures that Sheriff is heard long before he is seen

Tendency to backfire at high speeds

SHERIFF

Kerb feelers prevent wheel and fender damage

Red

The most caring, sharing and shy fire truck ever, Red spends every spare minute tending the flowers he plants in old tyres around town. At first he hates Lightning McQueen for trashing his garden and for the race car's big-shot attitude about Radiator Springs. But by the end of McQueen's time in the sleepy town, Red can't bear to see him leave!

Red has not one but two diesel engines: one to drive him to the fire, the other to power his water pump. His on-board water tank holds 3,785 litres (1,000 gallons) but he can suck up more from fire hydrants.

Official fire department emblem

Extra hose pipe lengths for those hard-to-reach plants and flowers

RADIATOR SPRINGS

Red's powerful hose is perfect for fighting fires – or watering the tailfin flowers and other plants he tends around town.

When Sally sees how dirty McQueen has become after working on the road, she asks Red to help out....

Good Citizen

Red is a fire truck of few words who is devoted to his community. In fact, he has a tendency to cry if someone speaks badly of it.

McQueen is surprised when Red hits him with a blast of cold water, but he's a lot cleaner afterwards!

The courthouse doubles as the firehouse. In years gone by, Red's siren and engine roar interrupted many court cases.

Red lives in the firehouse underneath the courthouse

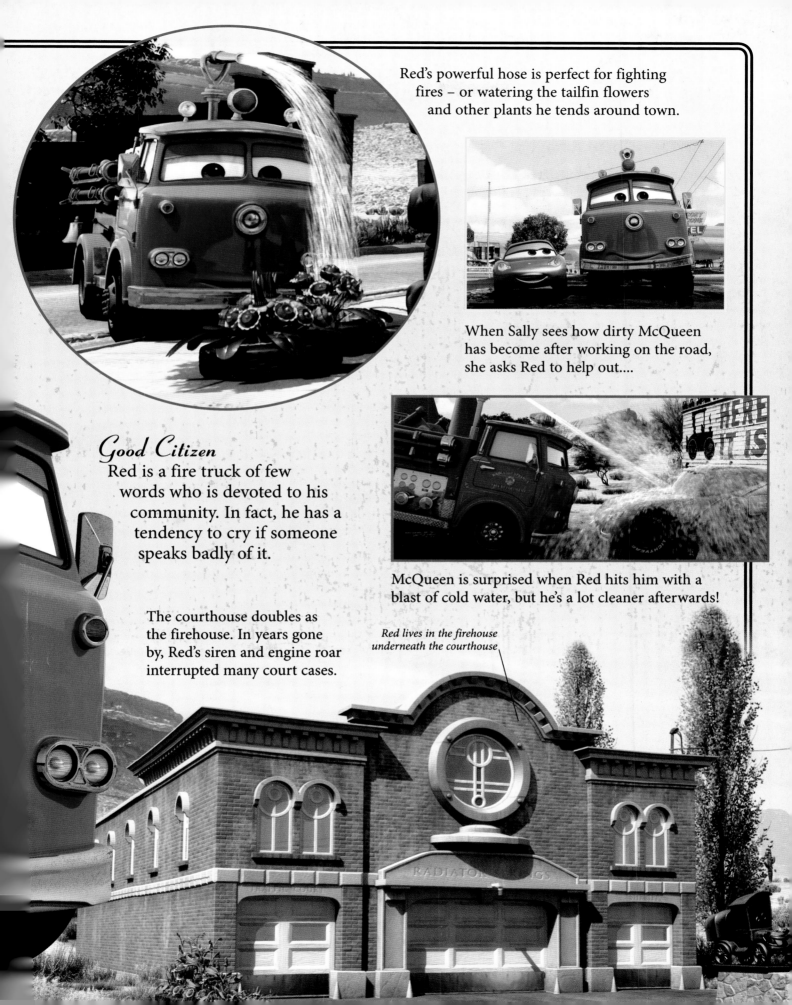

Luigi and Guido

Fiery, fast-talking Luigi and tyre-juggling forklift Guido followed their hearts from Italy to Radiator Springs, where they set up the town tyre shop, Luigi's Casa Della Tires. They are so proud of their Italian roots that they have even built their very own leaning tower... of tyres!

Luigi is crazy about autoracing. Meeting McQueen is a big thrill for him – until he learns McQueen doesn't know any Ferraris.

Luigi

Big-hearted and excitable, Luigi's enthusiasm and energy rubs off on everyone around him. He can't wait to fit out McQueen in a set of new whitewall tyres.

Fabric sun-roof

Fiat hood ornament

CAR FACTS

A tiny 500cc engine, 4-speed gearbox and a top speed of 60 mph (97 kph) means Luigi is nobody's speed machine, but wherever he goes, he arrives in style... and electrically powered Guido is never far behind.

Tyre stack imitates Italy's famous leaning Tower of Pisa

Customers who pull into the Casa Della Tires get more than just a new set of wheels. Luigi and Guido's lively personalities send them on their way with an extra spring in their suspension.

Everywhere you look – tyres!

There's always a sale at Luigi's

Luigi CASA DELLA TIRES

Guido

Guido dreams of performing a pit stop on a real race car. In fact, 'pit stop' is the only English the forklift knows.

uigi always recommends whitewalls to s customers. Black tyres blend into the vement. Whitewalls say look at me!

Lifting fork

Ferrari

At Willys Butte, Guido wears racing colours – Ferrari, of course!

Radiator Springs

For years, Radiator Springs' main street has been a sorry sight, so McQueen's repairs provide a much-needed facelift. Now everyone wants to enjoy a smooth cruise along the freshly laid blacktop. Folks have even been inspired to brighten up their shops!

Radiator Springs is the gateway to Ornament Valley

Red hosed down and cleaned the tower in honour of the new road...

...and Guido plans to put a new coat of paint on the Casa Della Tires

Luigi is quick to cruise along the smooth new road

Spring Cleaning

High-ridin' Ramone is Radiator Springs' paint-job artist, but he can paint more than just cars. Using his hydraulics and an airbrush, he makes quick work of sprucing up the white-picket fence in front of his and Flo's house.

Ramone's is the tallest building in Radiator Springs

Every store has been cleaned and preened

"Fantastico! É bellissimo!"

Ramone's body shop never looked brighter

Sarge

Old soldiers never die, they just open their own army surplus stores. Patriotic ex-army vehicle Sarge begins each day by raising the Stars and Stripes outside his store and playing Reveille, the rousing trumpet call heard each morning on every army base.

Sarge is hanging out at Flo's Café when McQueen's arrival provides some welcome excitement!

Sarge's shop is an old army Quonset hut, which is polished to a reflective sheen and set in a precisely manicured and super-neat lawn.

Sarge proudly raises the flag outside his store

CAR FACTS

Sarge's no-nonsense four-cylinder flathead 'Go Devil' engine has carried him across many battlefields and parade grounds. No terrain is too rough 'n' tough for his solid axles and thick-tread tyres!

Chunky tyres provide excellent grip for off-road driving

Sarge's neighbour Fillmore has a messy front yard, which the army car calls an 'untamed jungle'.

Shopping at Sarge's

Sarge's Surplus Hut stocks every kind of military gear. When Lightning McQueen drops in, Sarge tries to sell the race car a pair of night-vision goggles.

Team Player

Sarge's bark is worse than his bite, and when the town's residents form a pit crew for McQueen in the Piston Cup tie-breaker, he's one of the first to sign up.

Tough suspension withstands heavy impacts in combat

Fillmore

*L*aid-back camper van Fillmore believes in love and distrusts all forms of authority. He has a conspiracy theory for every occasion, but especially for why the major oil companies haven't switched over to ecologically friendly organic fuel.

Fillmore plans to add solar panels

Paintings are Fillmore's own design

Despite his distaste for authority, Fillmore still has a government-issued licence plate

MAY CARBURET
5123
COUNTY

Taste Test

Fillmore brews his own organic fuel in a variety of flavours. McQueen takes the taste test before leaving for the big race re-match and can't believe how good it is! He orders a case to take with him to the Piston Cup tie-breaker.

Fillmore's Dome and Backyard

Fillmore built his tie-dyed geodesic dome to a 1960s design. His free-flowin' backyard is the complete opposite of his neighbour Sarge's tidy hut and garden.

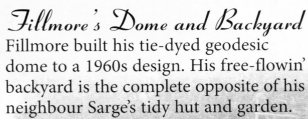

Muffler wind chimes

Tyre peace sign

Solar energy would make Fillmore's headlights more eco-friendly

Let It Be

Fillmore is a lover of the natural world. He lets his garden grow 'naturally' and believes in recycling. He made the wind chime above his gate from old mufflers and the peace sign from one of his old tyres.

Fillmore is convinced Sarge would be happier if he 'let the love in', but Sarge accuses him of being a hippie freak. The pair are always arguing, but can't live without each other.

Lizzie

Sprightly Lizzie is the town's oldest inhabitant – but she's got more gumption and 'horse-around' power than cars half her age. Her random comments keep the townsfolk on their toes, even though she can't often remember what she's just said. Lizzie takes quite a shine to Lightning McQueen.

Local Legend

Lizzie opened her shop back in the day and it has been open ever since. The shop doesn't just stock Highway 66 memorabilia... it has itself become a piece of the history of the Mother Road.

Lizzie is not a new model, but she has kept her curves!

Pneumatic tyre was state of the art... in 1923!

Whenever Lizzie starts thinking about the old times, she visits the statue of Stanley, the town's founder. She wishes Stanley could see how happy the town becomes after the new road is built.

Lizzie's Wares

McQueen is fascinated by Lizzie's motoring bric-a-brac, such as bumper stickers and souvenir snow globes.

One of Lizzie's snow globes is very special – it features a tiny, snow-covered model of her memorabilia shop!

Plain Speaker

Lizzie believes in telling it like it is, no matter what others might think. Her out-of-the-blue, straight-talking comments often surprise the younger inhabitants of Radiator Springs.

Squeaky front spring needs plenty of oil

Ramone

The sharpest-painted car in Radiator Springs, Ramone owns Ramone's House of Body Art – the finest custom body and paint shop for miles around. In fact, it's the only custom body and paint shop, but that doesn't take away from the fact that Ramone is an artist with an airbrush and a magician with paint and metal.

Body Shopping

Ramone's shop displays some of his latest hood designs in the windows. Flame job, ghost flames, even old-school pinstriping 'Von Dutch' style – Ramone will paint you up right.

CAR FACTS

Ramone has beefed-up his original Chevy small-block engine. He has also added headers, dual exhausts with glasspack mufflers and lots and lots of chrome including a chrome-plated undercarriage.

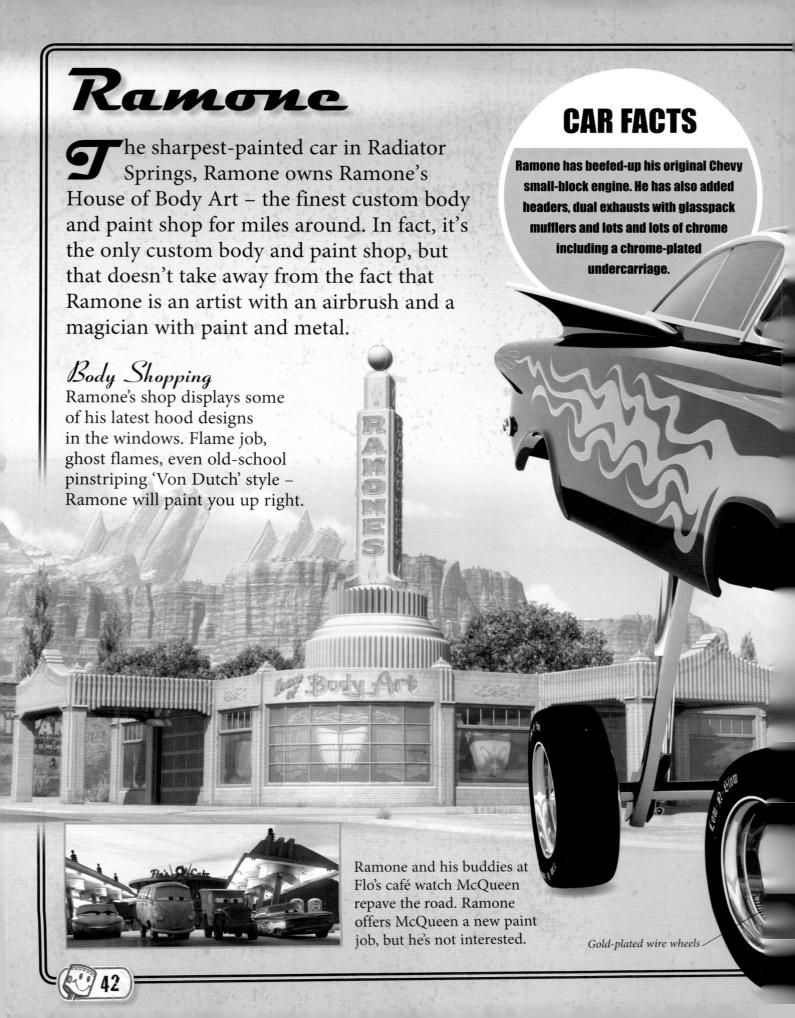

Ramone and his buddies at Flo's café watch McQueen repave the road. Ramone offers McQueen a new paint job, but he's not interested.

Gold-plated wire wheels

Quick-Change Artist!

It's been years since Ramone had a customer in his shop. But by re-painting himself daily, he has become his own best client and four-wheeled advertisement.

Ramone's favourite paint-job is always his latest paint-job!

Ramone's hydraulics let him ride high, low and everywhere in between

True Romantic

Ramone is married to Flo, a glamorous show car. He loves to switch his suspension to lower-than-low and cruise around town with Flo by his side.

Flo

Flo is a real looker – a 1950s show car who used to travel across the country, modelling her beautiful curves and swooping fins. One day she passed through Radiator Springs and fell in love with body artist extraordinaire Ramone. It was love at first sight for both of them, and she never left the little town.

When Mr. and Mrs. Mini Van pass through Radiator Springs, Flo offers them refreshment – but all they want are directions out of town!

CAR FACTS

Flo runs on a small block V-8 engine, but she is a good example of why you don't need a huge engine to turn heads. Flo's sumptuous curves and fantastic fins make her a true beauty.

Wise Wheels

Although sassy Flo may have a revved-up attitude, she's really a no-nonsense lady with the biggest heart in town. Her travels as a young, glamorous model have given her a store of experience and advice.

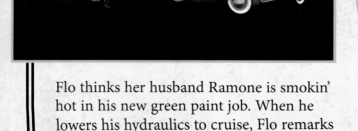

Flo thinks her husband Ramone is smokin' hot in his new green paint job. When he lowers his hydraulics to cruise, Flo remarks she hasn't seen him that low in years!

Swoopy bodywork

Elegant whitewall tyres

The V8 Café oozes style with its air filter-inspired hub

Wingnut centrepiece

Hanging Out

Flo's V8 Café offers 'the finest fuel in fifty states' and is everybody's favourite place to hang-out. The town's residents gather there every day to sip oil, gossip and collect pearls of wisdom from seen-it-all Flo.

Flo was known for her knock-out smile

A New Town

Sally tells McQueen about Radiator Springs'
glory days. The town was the most popular
stop on the old Highway 66. The shops were busy
and the café and motel stayed open late, greeting
travellers with their bright neon signs. So McQueen
enlists the help of Mater, Ramone and the others to
arrange a little surprise for Sally....

Luigi's tower of tyres glows from lights placed inside!

Wimpy's Wipers looks just like it did in its heyday

Luigi and Guido cruise Italian-style

A New Look

Sally is impressed with McQueen's new custom paint job from Ramone. In fact, McQueen helped everyone in town and became the best customer Radiator Springs had seen in a very long time.

The Lube-o-rama glows bright

Pinstripe-inspired neon on Ramone's House of Body Art

Blast from the Past

Cars cruise under the glow of the neon, just as they did long ago. Even the out-of-sync traffic light works just as it should.

LONDON, NEW YORK, MUNICH,
MELBOURNE AND DELHI

Senior Designer   Dan Bunyan
Project Editor   Neil Kelly
Designer   Lynne Moulding
Publishing Manager   Simon Beecroft
Brand Manager   Lisa Lanzarini
Category Publisher   Alex Allan
DTP Designer   Hanna Ländin
Production   Rochelle Talary

First published in Great Britain in 2006 by Dorling Kindersley Limited,
80 Strand, London, WC2R 0RL
A Penguin Company

06 07 08 10 9 8 7 6 5 4 3 2 1

A CIP catalogue record for this book is available from the British Library.

ISBN-13 978-1-40531-025-3   ISBN-10 1-4053-1025-1

Colour reproduction by Media Development and Printing Ltd, UK
Printed and bound by Toppan Printing Co. Ltd, China

ACKNOWLEDGMENTS
Dorling Kindersley would like to thank:
Krista Sheffler, Cherie Hammond, Leeann Alameda, Clay Welch, Desiree Mourad, Ed Chen, Jeff Raymond,
Kelly Bonbright, Jonathan Rodriguez and Jay Ward at Pixar Animation Studios; Lisa Gerstel, Graham Barnard,
and Tishana Williams at Disney Publishing; Heather Scott and Elizabeth Noble at Dorling Kindersley, for editorial help.

Discover more at
www.dk.com